Simply
Salvation

MARK FINLEY
with STEVEN MOSLEY

Pacific Press® Publishing Association
Nampa, Idaho
Oshawa, Ontario, Canada

Edited by B. Russell Holt
Cover design by Center Graphics Adventist Media Center
Typeset in 10/12 Century Schoolbook

Unless otherwise noted, all Scripture quotations are taken
from the New International Version.

ISBN 0-8163-1159-5

99 00 01 02 • 5 4 3 2

Contents

Introduction

I have conducted evangelistic meetings in the major cities of the world, with tens of thousands of people in attendance. Everywhere, people have basically the same questions. Some of those most frequently asked are:

"How can I be sure I have eternal life?"

"How can I know that my sins are forgiven?"

"What are the practical steps necessary to be saved?"

In five brief chapters, this little volume discusses how God reaches out and saves men and women. It clearly reveals how you can receive His gift of salvation. It will take you through a step-by-step process so you can know your sins are forgiven and that you have the gift of eternal life.

Why not begin each chapter with the prayer that Christ Himself will draw you close to Him? Salvation is not simply a matter of the mind; it is a matter of the heart. When the heart is open to the Spirit of God and you long to surrender your life to Him, He reveals Himself to you as the supreme Saviour.

These pages focus on Calvary. It was on the cross that the sinless, divine Son of God assumed the responsibility for the sins of the whole world. It was on the cross that Christ revealed His love for the human race. This volume will lead you to the cross. Thousands have come here before you. And here, in imagination, they have seen the nails driven into His hands, the crown of thorns thrust upon His head, and the spear pierce His side. At the cross, they have witnessed this matchless love. Your heart will be drawn to the One who loves you so much.

My associate, Steven Mosley, and I will be earnestly praying that the Spirit of God will touch your life and that you will be led into the arms of our loving Saviour as you read these pages.

—Mark Finley

Between Rescue and the Sea

They found his skeleton beside a makeshift shelter on the beach, near the pounding surf of the mid-Atlantic. He'd tried to survive alone on a desolate island called Ascension. Beside the body was a journal that told one of the most remarkable stories in seafaring history. Here was a second Robinson Crusoe who waited for rescue and found, instead, his own private hell.

"By order of the commodore and captains of the Dutch fleet I was set on shore the 5th of May, 1725, upon the Island of Ascension, which struck me with great dread and uneasiness, having no hope remaining but that the Almighty God would be my protector." So begins the journal of an anonymous seaman's four-month ordeal. Some terrible crime had caused the authorities to abandon him on this desolate island with only a cask of water, a hatchet, a teakettle, a tarp, and a few other items.

The man quickly set up a tent and began foraging for food. He felt terribly abandoned, of course, but kept climbing the hills each day in hope of spotting some stray ship. Within a few days, he managed to locate a tiny stream high amid the rocks. He was also able to catch birds and turtles to eat along with the rice that he had been given.

But as May turned into June, and June into July, water

became more scarce on the island. The seaman spotted some mountain goats on one of his wanderings and followed them to a few pools of water in the rocks. But these steadily dwindled. Soon there was no water to be found anywhere. The man was reduced to drinking the blood of the turtles he killed with his hatchet, and then to drinking seawater, even though this was deadly. His last journal entry reads: "I am becoming a moving skeleton; my strength is entirely decayed; I cannot write much longer."

This anonymous seaman endured great physical suffering during his grueling struggle to survive. But there was a much greater pain that stood out, something repeated throughout his journal. And that was his consuming guilt.

He wrote mournfully, "Night is an emblem of my crimes and each clear day renews my punishment." Later he exclaimed in the journal: "What pangs, alas, do wretched mortals feel who headstrong tread the giddy maze of life and leave the beauteous paths of righteousness."

In his desolation and deprivation, the seaman's guilt began to take on a voice and a form. He was tormented by blasphemous curses and vile expressions that erupted in the dead of night—out of nowhere. He began to see frightening apparitions. The vast, faceless sea imprisoning him permitted no rescue. His hours spent gazing out at the horizon in vain sank him ever more deeply into despair. He was all alone in the universe; no one would ever come for him.

In the end, the tortured man succumbed. What is most haunting are the words regarding his past, his unerasable past: "My crime was of the blackest dye; nor could I possibly form an idea in my mind of a punishment that could make the least atonement for so great an offense."

There's nothing in this world quite as isolating as guilt. The punishment this nameless prisoner received would be considered cruel and unusual today. It probably was back then, as well. But it gives us a picture of one of our deepest problems—guilt, inescapable guilt.

In recent years, pop psychology has tried its best to rid us of this chronic problem. We've been assured that we're no worse than the next person; that guilt feelings are just feelings, and we can choose other ones; that we must accept the way we are unconditionally. Bestsellers have promoted sex without guilt. Self-fulfillment without guilt. Assertiveness without guilt. Looking out for number one without guilt. Well-meaning people have done their best to sweep guilt right off the horizon. The message we're getting is that guilt is simply a mistake.

Well, if it's a mistake, it's one that we keep right on making. Guilt doesn't go away, however much we try to massage the psyche.

Why?

One of the principal reasons is this: We keep trying to deal with the symptoms instead of the root problem. We want to anesthetize those unpleasant feelings instead of facing their sources. So, of course, those feelings keep coming up again. I'd like to suggest that there was one Physician of the soul who dealt with the problem thoroughly—at the root. There was only one Man in history who offered a realistic rescue.

Let's look first at His diagnosis; we find it in the Gospel of John. Jesus is pointing out man's basic problem to a Pharisee named Nicodemus. He says, "Light has come into the world, but men loved darkness instead of light because their deeds were evil. Everyone who does evil hates the light, and will not come into the light for fear that his deeds will be exposed" (John 3:19, 20). Through these words, Jesus is explaining why some people will be condemned even though He came into the world to save us, not condemn us. It's because people turn away from the light, God's truth; they are afraid of being exposed.

Notice that the issue is not how much good or how much bad we have inside us. It's taken for granted that we all make mistakes; we all do things that make us feel guilty. The issue is how we respond when the solution comes. When God wants to shine His light inside us, do we honestly confess what's there? Or do we go off in a corner to hide? Guilt can never be solved until we acknowledge that we have sinned.

We deserve to feel guilty, of course. We break the law of God, the law of the universe. Guilt is not something to try to sweep under the carpet; it's a sign pointing us toward the cure. People have a chronic problem with guilt only if they keep ignoring the sign.

The Bible tells us we're all on an island, surrounded by a hostile sea. Sin has separated us from God. We need rescue. As that nameless seaman on the island of Ascension realized with a pang: "The wages of sin is death" (Romans 6:23). We can't survive on our barren island; we need a reconciliation with God. Yet our sin is precisely what isolates us from Him.

What's the solution to our dilemma? The answer is beautifully illustrated by one of history's epic voyages. During one of Sir Ernest Shackleton's attempts to cross the Antarctic Ocean in 1914, his ship, the *Endurance*, was crushed in an ice floe. The crew drifted for days until they could make a landing on Elephant Island.

Shackleton had the men set up camp there where they could preserve their supplies and try to survive the coming winter. But he soon realized that no one would be coming to rescue them. No one had any idea where they were. They were cut off from the world by the freezing, stormy Antarctic Ocean. There was only one hope of rescue: Someone had to cross that hostile ocean and get help. Shackleton began to rig a twenty-foot whaling boat for the voyage. From volunteers, he picked a crew of six. They would have to cross eight hundred miles of tempestuous sea in order to reach a Norwegian whaling station on the frozen island of South Georgia.

It seemed an impossible task in an open boat at the stormiest time of year. But Shackleton set out with his men. For days they huddled under a makeshift canvas covering, keeping the bow turned into the fiercest waves, praying that the wind wouldn't tear their small sail away. They endured bone-chilling cold, sleeping bags frozen stiff, icy water streaming down their backs, hunger, and thirst. Fourteen days after their voyage began, when all were almost dead of exposure and thirst, they spotted the black cliffs of South Georgia! Shackleton had made it through; soon a ship would be on its way to rescue the rest of his stranded men.

When God looked down at our predicament and saw that we were isolated on our island, surrounded by a boundless sea of sin, He plunged into that hostile sea Himself. He took on Himself the murderous, icy vastness of the evil in humankind.

Come with me to a rocky garden called Gethsemane. Jesus is praying there in agony, fully aware of the ordeal ahead of Him. Will Christ willingly submit to the horror of the cross? Will He risk the unthinkable—eternal separation from the Father? Christ, alone and prostrate in Gethsemane, was a little like Shackleton staring out into the forbidding Antarctic Ocean. To take his tiny boat into its midst meant almost certain death. Yet that was the only way he could hope to save his men.

Jesus, too, realized that there was only one way to save humanity from the penalty of sin; He had to absorb the sentence of death in His own body; He had to take on the agonies of hell. And so, with trembling lips, the Saviour said, " 'Father, . . . not my will, but yours be done' " (Luke 22:42). Listen as the footsteps of a mob approach. Their bobbing torches flash in the dark. Judas approaches Jesus; he says, "Hail Master," and betrays Him with a kiss.

Suddenly, the divine Son of God is pushed into the crowd. They spit at His face and yank at His beard. A fist strikes Him in the eye; a slap stings His face. This is the very One whose name angels carry to galaxies afar, singing, "Holy, holy, holy." This is the One who hung the worlds in space. But now a sweaty, cursing, cruel mob takes Him in their calloused hands.

Come with me to Pilate's judgment hall. False witnesses come forward to accuse Him. He is despised and mocked. The spotless, innocent Lamb of God is sentenced as a guilty offender. He is condemned for sins He never committed so that I can have my well-deserved guilt removed. He is tried and convicted so that I can be tried and acquitted.

Come with me to Pilate's courtyard. A muscular Roman raises his thick arm. Listen to the snap of the whip. Watch as Jesus' back is torn and the blood flows down His back. Many men who went through this scourging were all but disemboweled. Jesus—the One who existed with the Father from all eternity; the One worshiped by countless angels—was wounded for our transgressions, just as the prophet Isaiah had predicted. He was bruised for our iniquities. He took the blows that we should have taken; the chastisement of our peace is upon Him; and with His stripes we are healed (see Isaiah 53:4-7).

Come with me to a hill called Calvary. A crown of thorns is shoved down on His head. Spikes are driven through His hands and feet—into a cross. The instrument of execution is lifted up and falls with a thud into its hole. Tissues and tendons and muscles tear. His limbs are pulled out of joint; He feels as though He is suffocating.

But strange as it may seem, this physical torture is drowned out by something else. Another kind of pain consumes this isolated man. We hear it in His dark cry:

"'My God, my God, why have you forsaken me?'" (Matthew 27:46). Jesus experiences in those moments the most horrendous abandonment possible—eternal separation from God. As He suffers, He evidently cannot see through the darkness of the tomb; He does not see Himself rising victorious in the resurrection.

But still, He is willing to go into the grave—even if He never comes out. He does that so you and I can be with His Father forever. Jesus is willing to give up His place in heaven so that you and I can sit on His throne.

I can't imagine love like that. I can't grasp the enormity of Christ's sacrifice. I can only gaze in wonder at those scenes that make vivid the words of John: "'For God so loved the world that he *gave* his one and only Son'" (John 3:16, emphasis supplied). But once in a while, here on our sin-darkened planet, we get a tiny glimpse of what such a sacrifice really means.

On February 3, 1943, the *S.S. Dorchester* was torpedoed in the North Atlantic. This transport ship, filled with American soldiers, took on water rapidly and began listing to starboard. Everything on board was sheer chaos. The radio had been knocked out. Men rushed around on the ragged edge of panic. Many had run up from the hold without life jackets. Overcrowded lifeboats capsized; rafts drifted away before anyone could reach them. Survivors would later testify that there seemed only one little island of order in all the confusion—the spot where four chaplains stood on the steeply sloping starboard side.

These four, George Lansing Fox, a pastor from Chicago; Alexander David Goode, a rabbi from New York City; Clark Poling, a minister from Schenectady, New York; and John Washington, a priest from New Jersey, were calmly guiding men to their boat stations. They distributed life jackets from a storage locker and then helped men frozen with fear over the side.

One survivor recalls hearing the noise of hundreds of men crying, pleading, praying, swearing. But through it all the chaplains spoke words of courage and confidence. "Their voices were the only thing that kept me going," he said.

When the supply of life jackets was gone, the four chaplains gave away their own. One of the last men to get off the ship as the deck was flooding looked back and saw the chaplains still standing firm, their arms linked, braced against the slanting deck. Across the waves their voices still sounded, praying in Latin, Hebrew, and English. As one seaman put it, "It was the finest thing I have ever seen, or hope to see, this side of heaven."

Friends, this side of heaven, we have to pause in awe and look back at the One who went down with the ship for us. Those chaplains were willing to plunge into the icy, dark waters of the North Atlantic so that a few more young men could live. Jesus was willing to disappear forever into the darkness, consumed by sin, in order to give every human being eternal life. Jesus is standing on the deck of our sinking ship—handing out life jackets. He knows He's going down with the ship, but He wants to make sure that each of us has life.

The Bible's best-known text says, " 'For God so loved the world that he gave his one and only Son, that whoever believes in him shall not perish but have eternal life' " (John 3:16). The promise is for "whoever." Rich, poor, young, old —everyone. Whether you're good or bad or somewhere in between, you need a life jacket. And Jesus is passing them out to whomever.

You don't have to perish in the icy sea, isolated from the Father. Thank God that we don't have to bear our guilt alone like that tortured seaman on the island of Ascension. No, we can't atone for our sins; we can't make up for our mistakes. But, yes, the penalty has been paid. The vastness of the sea of sin has been crossed; our rescue is at hand.

From the cross, Jesus is able to tell us, "You don't have to perish. You can have the gift of everlasting life. Come to Me and confess your sins. Accept My rescue; I've come such a long way, and gone through so much, to give it to you."

Accept the gift of amazing grace that the Saviour offers us as we pray.

* * *

"Father in heaven, we're weary of trying to survive on our little island. We can't deal with our guilt alone. There's no remedy for the sickness in our souls. And so we come to the cross, where You have created a cure at such great cost. Thank You for bridging the murderous sea of sin. Thank You for the gift of grace. Thank You for laying Your body down so that we may cross safely into the arms of our Father. We confess our sins, our indifference, our ill will. Thank You for reaching out to us in grace. Thank You for pardon and reconciliation and acceptance. We place our faith in You as Saviour and Lord. We dedicate our lives to You. Thank You for taking us—just now, just as we are. In the name of Jesus Christ, Amen."

Holding God
for Ransom

On a Tuesday evening, March 1, 1932, Bruno Hauptmann, a Bronx carpenter, quietly leaned a long ladder against the second-story window of a lovely villa on Sourland Mountain, New Jersey.

Bruno was not there to make repairs on the house. He had a different mission in mind. He managed to climb the ladder making very little noise. He opened the window shutters without difficulty, since they were warped and couldn't be bolted shut, then slipped inside the bedroom.

The world's attention would soon be focused on what happened inside that bedroom. A clear answer would never emerge. But very shortly, Bruno Hauptmann climbed back through the window and began descending the ladder. He had a tiny bundle in one arm, a baby boy nicknamed "Buster," whom his parents also affectionately called our "fat little lamb."

In a few days, it seemed that all the world was swept up in this one family's tragedy. For this baby was Charles Lindbergh, Jr., and he would never see his parents again.

Charles and Anne Lindbergh seemed to lead an idyllic existence at their isolated hideaway near Hopewell, New Jersey. They were probably the most celebrated couple of their time. Charles Lindbergh had earned international renown with his solo flight in the *Spirit of St. Louis* over the Atlantic Ocean. He was now quite financially successful as a leader in the new airline industry. Charles and Anne were devoted to each other and to their son; the couple enjoyed flying together and took several adventurous trips to different parts of the world.

They had also just completed their dream house—the family hideaway on Sourland Mountain, safe from prying eyes and curious crowds.

The Lindberghs had everything. But then on that Tuesday night, at 10:00 p.m., Mrs. Lindbergh heard a knock on her bedroom door. One of the servants asked, "Do you have the baby?" It wasn't in its crib.

Not yet alarmed, they went to ask Charles in the library if he had the baby. He did not. Bounding up the stairs, the father burst into the bedroom to find the crib empty, the imprint of the child's body still on the mattress and pillow. And stuck to the windowsill was an envelope with a ransom note inside.

Charles had to tell his wife, "Anne, they have stolen our baby."

All she could say was, "It isn't possible." Even in the darkest hour, neither could imagine the ordeal that lay ahead.

On occasion the Lindberghs had talked about the worst thing that could happen to them, the thing that could shatter their island of bliss. And both knew what it was. They were most vulnerable through their child. Through the tragedy of the Lindbergh family, I'd like to take a look at a wider tragedy, one we're all involved in.

Did you ever stop to think that God Almighty might be vulnerable in a similar way? Have you ever imagined that God Himself could be kidnapped and held for ransom? In this chapter, we're going to gain a glimpse into the very heart of God the Father.

When news flashed out that the Lindbergh baby had been kidnapped, everyone wanted to know more. This was the biggest story American newspapers had ever dealt with. The public demanded news of the search for the missing child. Some of the big-city tabloids actually manufactured news. They came out with headlines such as "Lindy's Baby Found," "Blood Money Paid," or "Tot Released."

Adding to the parents' agony was the insensitivity, and sometimes outright cruelty, of countless people fascinated by the kidnapping. Letters poured into the Lindbergh home by the thousands. Many offered sympathy. But many others actually gloated over the Lindberghs' misery, writing to say that this tragedy was God's wrath, a just punishment for their sins of pride, arrogance, and affluence.

Some people managed to discover the family's private telephone number. They would call in the night to say they had the child or knew where he was hidden—and then laugh and jeer or mutter obscenities.

Then there were the politicians and film stars who decided this spectacular crime might yield them some good publicity. Several announced they were coming to Hopewell, where the Lindberghs lived, to reveal important clues about the kidnapper or the missing child. They would arrive with much fanfare, speak some vague nonsense to newspaper reporters, and then demand to be photographed with the Lindberghs, to show, they said, "how much we sympathize."

All this, of course, only intensified the parents' pain and anguish. The loss of their "fat little lamb" was bad enough, but the whole world seemed to be magnifying it, tearing at the wounds. So, naturally, the Lindberghs withdrew more and more from all contact with outsiders.

This crime brought to the surface something dark and cruel in human nature. Why? What is this ugliness inside us? Let me take you to another scene, another kidnapping, where we can get at the root of the problem of human cruelty.

God Himself was once kidnapped and held for ransom. The crime took place on a hill called Golgotha, the Place of the Skull. God the Son, the Lamb without blemish, was crying out in anguish while crucified on a Roman cross. His limbs pierced, His back shredded, a crown of thorns beaten down on His head, the Son shouted, "'My God, my God, why have you forsaken me?'" (Matthew 27:46).

He was feeling the horror of ultimate and eternal separation from God the Father. The innocent victim, God the one and only Son, was dying a horrible death. And what did the bystanders do? Those fellow countrymen who had listened to Him speak unforgettable words and watched Him perform wonders—how did they react to the crime? Matthew, an eyewitness, tells us:

> Those who passed by hurled insults at him, shaking their heads and saying, "You who are going to destroy the temple and build it in three days, save yourself! Come down from the cross, if you are the Son of God!" (Matthew 27:39, 40).

Was it just the ruffians of Jerusalem who came to gloat over some poor wretch's suffering? Was it only the worst among men who engaged in this cruel mockery? No, the "best" classes of society joined in too: "In the same way the chief priests, the teachers of the law and the elders mocked him. 'He saved others,' they said, 'but he can't save himself!'" (verses 41, 42).

Here are the elite, the leaders of that society, men schooled in lofty religious principles—all viciously mocking a man being tortured to death.

Why? Why would anyone want to add to such suffering?

Why would anyone want to add to the torment of the Lindberghs?

There is something inside human beings that can drive us to such cruelty. In the case of the chief priests and elders, it was simple jealousy. Jesus was their big rival. They were so intent on protecting their status, their turf, that they actually persuaded themselves that this spotless Lamb of God was worthy of the cruelest execution.

That's the human tragedy. We know in our hearts about right and wrong. We feel an obligation to love our fellow man. But there's another principle at work in our hearts as well. Other forces drive us to say cruel things, to remain indifferent to suffering, to hurt the ones we love the most.

The wonder is that God allowed Himself to be swept up in our tragedy. He willingly absorbed the toxic effects of sin in His own body on the cross. He took on our guilt and shame. The Lamb of God was sacrificed for our moral failings.

Jesus was kidnapped by the mindless cruelty of sin. He was held for ransom—and paid that ransom with His own life so that we could go free.

But, you may wonder, where was God the Father in all this? What role did He play in the tragedy? A look at Charles Lindbergh's search for his child gives us a picture.

One day this distraught father received a visit from John Curtis, a Virginia boat builder. The man seemed sympathetic, high-minded, and genuinely eager to help. Curtis told Lindbergh that he had come across the captain of a vessel in which the baby was being held.

Once again, hope sprang up in the hearts of Anne and Charles Lindbergh. Would they at last be reunited with their beloved child? Curtis hired a boat and set off to sea one night with Charles for a secret rendezvous with the ship holding the boy. But they missed the boat.

The next night the two set out again to find it—but again

missed the rendezvous. They did this for three whole weeks. And each night Curtis convinced Charles that because of bad weather or crossed signals, they had just missed the connection and would have to try again the next evening. Curtis sounded so sincere, so public-spirited.

The two men were out on the ocean the night of May 12, 1932, with Charles leaning out over the bow, intently scouring the dark waves for the ship, when a news bulletin flashed over their radio. A truck driver, stopping along the road to Princeton, had noticed what appeared to be a shallow grave. He nudged at the dirt with his foot and laid bare a child's hand. Digging quickly, he uncovered the body of Charles Lindbergh, Jr. The child's skull had been crushed.

That's how this father learned about his baby's fate. Out in the dark, helplessly searching the ocean for his lost child. His desperate search turned out to be a cruel hoax. John Curtis had made the whole thing up.

Some people, in looking at Calvary, have pictured God the Father as a vindictive Being of boundless wrath whose fury against the sins of humankind can be placated only by the intercession of the loving Jesus. God the Father is wrath; God the Son is mercy—that's how we sometimes see it.

But as a matter of fact, the sacrifice of the Father was every bit as great as that of the Son. Jesus wasn't the only one who suffered on that fateful day. God the Father suffered as well; He had made the ultimate sacrifice of a Father—giving up His Son.

As God looked down from heaven on the tragedy at Calvary, the hardest thing for Him to take must have been the knowledge of what He could have done, but wouldn't do. Think of it. God Almighty enthroned at the center of the universe, sovereign over all, with countless angels waiting to do His bidding. And yet He couldn't lift a finger to save His only begotten Son. He had to stand on the sidelines while the Son was beaten, mocked, and crucified.

Why? Because there was no other way for humankind to be rescued from the great tragedy of sin.

Like Charles Lindbergh staring out into the vast, empty ocean in search of his lost boy, God had searched for some other way, some other solution. But there was none. He Himself would have to make the ultimate sacrifice.

So if you think that God reluctantly shows mercy only because the Son talks Him into it, think again. He was willing to give up everything for us. It says so right in the most famous verse in the Bible. It's so familiar we sometimes miss the main point. Listen. " '*God* loved the world so much that he gave his only Son, that everyone who has faith in him may not die but have eternal life' " (John 3:16, NEB, emphasis supplied).

Why did Jesus die? Because God loved the world so much. So much that He was willing to tear Himself away from His own Son during those wrenching hours on Golgotha and leave Him to die in our place.

He heard the news from afar, as it were, like a radio crackling on some ship drifting in the night: The Son had been found, broken, cruelly murdered.

This, however, brings us to another question. If God the Father was indeed eager to forgive us from the beginning, if He was eager to show mercy even before Christ died, why did the sacrifice have to be made? Why go through with this terrible ordeal?

Again, a look at something that happened to the Lindberghs gives us a clue.

The trial of Bruno Hauptmann for the murder of Charles Lindbergh, Jr., had just concluded with the judge's summation to the jury. Several years had passed since the night of the kidnapping. Mr. Lindbergh rushed home to tell Anne and a few other close friends that the jury was deliberating. The couple seemed calm. But Charles Lindbergh's health had suffered from the strain of the long trial. He was coughing continually.

Anne and Charles knew that news of the verdict would come over the radio. So they kept two sets on as they ate dinner in strained silence. Afterward they looked through family albums and pretended to study the pictures, though their minds were far away.

Suddenly the news flashed on. Hauptmann had been condemned to death. Anne's face turned white; she and her husband rushed over and turned up the radio. A reporter was speaking outside the courtroom. In the background, one could hear the yelling of a huge crowd, eager for blood. The reporter said, "You have now heard the verdict in the most famous trial in all history. Bruno Hauptmann now stands guilty of the foulest . . ."

They turned the radio off. They'd heard enough. A little later Charles told a friend, "My one dread all these years has been that they would get hold of someone as a victim about whom I wasn't sure. I am sure about this—quite sure." Then he proceeded to go over the case point by point with the group gathered there. It was his way of easing the terrible tension they'd been living under. But it also fulfilled a deeper need. Charles reviewed the evidence carefully, putting all the pieces together, showing how they all pointed to Hauptmann, showing why he was guilty—beyond a reasonable doubt.

A friend listening recalled later, "It was very well done. It made one feel that here was no personal desire for vengeance or justification; here was the solemn process of law inexorably punishing a culprit."

Charles reminded them all of the terrifying yells of the people outside the courthouse, and he said, "That was a lynching crowd."

God the Father also had to listen to the horrible sounds of a lynching crowd—one gathered around His dying Son.

He had nothing in common with their cries for blood. But God does have a concern with justice, with law, with moral values. Something inside God compelled Him to go over the case point by point, making sure that He could, as Paul tells us, remain just and yet the justifier of repentant sinners.

God, in the person of the Son, had to assume the role of the guilty party and absorb in Himself the deadly results of sin. Only in this way could He stand in our place as our Substitute and pay the ransom that frees us from the condemnation of the law. Paul expresses this very clearly in 2 Corinthians 5:21: "God made him [Jesus] who had no sin to be sin for us, so that in him we might become the righteousness of God."

But, we may ask, who was the ransom for? Who was the penalty paid to? God's law, justice, honor, the moral order? These things are important. But here's the main point: God's justice and His law aren't separate from God, something standing over Him to which He owes an obligation. They are a part of His nature, of who He is.

Charles Lindbergh, because of the kind of person he was, *had* to know that justice had been served in the verdict of Bruno Hauptmann. He *had* to be assured that the trial was fair.

In a similar way God was satisfying Himself in the atonement. God is inherently just, fair, honorable, and truthful. He will not—He cannot—contradict Himself. God could not forgive sins without expressing His wrath against sin, without accepting the consequences. He Himself would take on the burden of humanity's indifference and cruelty.

Now admittedly, some of us are uncomfortable relating these legal terms to salvation. We can't imagine a loving heavenly Father active in a courtroom setting. But God has always sought to assure us of His commitment in covenant terms, legal terms. That doesn't make Him some stern judge tied up in an arbitrary system of law.

Think about a couple who has fallen in love; they want to be together forever. They will seek a legally recognized marriage. Do we accuse them of having an immature love because they bring legal issues into their relationship? Of course not. Their legal, public declaration demonstrates the depth of their affection.

In the same way, the One lifted up as a spectacle on the cross demonstrates the depths of His love. He gives us clear grounds for security—covenant security. He doesn't just toss us the cheap forgiveness of someone who says, "It's OK; forget it." He pardons full and free; He justifies us; He declares us righteous in His sight—at great cost to Himself.

Are you ready to accept the pardon God offers you so freely? Are you ready to seek His solution to the tragedy of the sin principle working within you?

Open your mind and your heart right now to the One who was willing to pay the ultimate price, go through the ultimate ordeal, for your redemption. God allowed Himself to be kidnapped and cruelly murdered. Now He wants to adopt you as His new son or daughter. Now He wants to welcome you into eternal life with Him.

* * *

"Loving Father, thank You for taking a stand for us on Calvary. We ourselves now stand in its shadow. Cover us with Your pardon. We gratefully receive the gift of a right standing with You. We thank You for accepting us completely in Jesus Christ. Help us to live each day in the light of Your love. Amen."

Death by Design

Dallas, Texas. November 22, 1963. Black Friday.

Just six shattering seconds on that sunny afternoon in Dallas, and a president was dead. Who committed the awful crime? Three decades later, we are more confused than ever.

First word of the tragic shooting of President Kennedy came when the news bulletins interrupted the routine dilemmas of the soap operas. Then came the terrible confirmation—the president was dead!

The stock market shut down. Newscasters couldn't control their emotions. People sobbed in the streets. The world was stunned, bewildered, brokenhearted. In six short seconds, our world was shattered, and it has never been quite the same since. Life went on, but the questions lingered. Most troubling of all: "Who did it?" Did Lee Harvey Oswald act alone? Was there a conspiracy?

Many of us remember exactly where we were and what we were doing when we heard the news that Kennedy had been shot. That event shocked a whole generation. For quite a few people, it became a turning point in their lives and in how they viewed their country. John Kennedy had brought a certain youthful exuberance and optimism to the office of the presidency. Many Americans felt inspired to "ask not what your country can do for you, but what you can do for your country."

Today, in the United States we're surrounded by what appear to be insurmountable problems: a budget deficit bigger than anyone can grasp; inner cities that no one seems able to rescue from violence and poverty; global threats to the environment. Government seems all but immobilized. As a result, many people look back with nostalgia on the idealism that seemed to characterize Kennedy's presidency. Back then, *politics* wasn't such a dirty word. Those bullets ringing out in Dallas seem to have brought to an end our age of innocence.

Perhaps you're wondering, "Is it still possible to dream in our world?" "Can we still cling to ideals?" "Do the best and brightest always end up trampled on by the worst?"

Let me tell you about another black Friday long ago when another charismatic leader was assassinated. Because in His story we find the answers to these questions—and much more.

This Man, like Kennedy, brought a certain youthful exuberance to His life calling. He also promised to lead His people into a new frontier, the kingdom of God. And He sparked hope and idealism in a society dominated by a rigid, conservative hierarchy.

Jesus of Nazareth flashed like a brilliant light through the hills of Judea and the fields of Galilee; He electrified crowds wherever He went. And then, after three short years, it was all over. On a black Friday in Jerusalem, His enemies crucified Him. It's been nearly two thousand years since Jesus died. After all this time, questions still linger in the minds of many, the same questions we wrestle with regarding the death of John Kennedy. Who killed Him? Who killed Jesus?

Were the Romans guilty? To some degree, certainly. Crucifixion was a Roman method of execution. It was the

Roman governor who signed the death decree. It was Roman soldiers who actually nailed Jesus to the cross. Yes, the Romans had their part to play in the death of Christ.

So did the religious establishment of that day. Jesus came to the Jews as their Messiah, but they refused to accept Him. "He came to His own, and His own did not receive Him" (John 1:11, NKJV). Instead of welcoming their Messiah, the Jewish leaders determined to put Him to death.

After numerous attempts failed, they finally recognized an opportunity when Judas offered to betray Him. Pilate, the Roman governor, was reluctant to sentence Jesus to die; he looked for an easy way out. But the Jewish leaders persisted. At last they won their case and arranged the death of their Messiah.

During the centuries since then, Jewish people have often borne the total blame for Christ's death. Early Christian church fathers condemned them. Medieval crusaders drove their swords through them. Inquisitors tormented them. Finally came Hitler's Holocaust. The sad truth is that many so-called Christians didn't feel too bad about what happened to all those Jews; after all, hadn't they killed Jesus?

But wait a moment. The fact is that every human being who has ever lived had a part to play in the death of Jesus. It was for *our* sins that He died.

> He was wounded for our transgressions, He was bruised for our iniquities; the chastisement for our peace was upon Him, and by His stripes we are healed. All we like sheep have gone astray; we have turned, every one, to his own way; and the Lord has laid on Him the iniquity of us all (Isaiah 53:5, 6, NKJV).

It is absolutely essential for us to understand the truth about Christ's death and how He can help us cling to the ideals of His kingdom amid the challenges of life.

So who was responsible for the death of Jesus? The Jewish leaders masterminded it. The Romans played their part. You and I, because we are sinners, bear responsibility as well. But the surprising truth is this: Nobody actually killed Jesus! That's right, nobody took away Christ's life from Him. He made that clear:

> "I am the good shepherd; and I know My sheep, and am known by My own. . . . I lay down My life for the sheep. . . . No one takes it from Me, but I lay it down of Myself. I have power to lay it down, and I have power to take it again" (John 10:14, 15, 18, NKJV).

According to Jesus, nobody took His life away from Him; nobody killed Him. Being the Good Shepherd, He laid down His life of His own free will. He chose to become a redemptive sacrifice. Here's where the assassination of John Kennedy and the crucifixion of Jesus Christ come into sharp contrast. Kennedy's death was a tragic loss; it simply left a hole in the life of the nation. The death of Christ was a glorious accomplishment. His idealistic kingdom didn't end on Calvary; it began there. That's where a new era of innocence begins. That's where weak, sinful human beings can find forgiveness and a new start.

Both the killing of John Kennedy and the killing of Jesus Christ were deaths by design. Evil men wanted to destroy them both. But the amazing thing in Jesus' case is this: He participated in the design of His own death. Working together with God the Father, He fashioned that cruel ordeal in such a way that it would create atonement, redemption, and reconciliation for all human beings.

Admittedly, sometimes Christ's legacy seems pretty watered down. Christianity doesn't appear to be quite the revolutionary force it once was. Many people view churches as champions only of the status quo. And they wonder if what we need isn't a new source of spiritual power. Even if Christ's death was heroic, they say, perhaps He exists today only as a comforting myth.

John F. Kennedy, by most accounts, grew in popularity considerably after his death. He has become, in many people's minds, almost a mythical figure—the last politician who really cared. What most people remember are his ideals, set forth in eloquent speeches.

But what about Christ? Is that all He is today? A man who cared, but who lives today only in the ideals of the Sermon on the Mount?

To answer these questions, I'd like to tell you about an assassin, a killer—Tex Watson. This man was even more disturbed than Lee Harvey Oswald, and he seemed headed toward the same sad fate.

In the early sixties, Tex traveled to southern California in search of total freedom. He began hanging around an abandoned movie ranch with members of Charles Manson's "family." Tex proved to be a great pupil, absorbing great quantities of drugs and Manson philosophy. Manson told his disciples that they must be free like wild animals to live, lie, and kill.

What followed was the Tate-La Bianca bloodbath in the summer of 1969. The nation was shocked at the calculated madness with which seven people were butchered. Tex was convicted as one of the murderers. Psychiatrists diagnosed him as "insane, totally incapable of standing trial." While in the Los Angeles County jail, he would throw himself, screaming, against the bars. At times his behavior was so destructive he had to be bound in a hospital bed.

Today, visitors can find Tex in a medium-security prison

at San Luis Obispo, California. But what they see is in striking contrast to some other members of the Manson family, who still seem deranged after all these years. Visitors discover a cheerful, clear-eyed man leading Bible studies with other inmates and sensitively answering their questions. Tex Watson, it turns out, is now the hard-working head of Abounding Love Ministries.

Now, jailhouse conversions often seem too convenient to be true. But Tex has held "model-prisoner" status for fifteen years. A chaplain who has worked with him for some time says, "This is the kind of total spiritual revolution that only comes through the powerful and loving work of the Holy Spirit, bringing new life to the human heart."

What happened to the man known as "Charles Manson's executioner"? He met the living Christ. He met the charismatic Leader who is far more than a comforting myth. Tex says this about the encounter: "I began to see that even for a guilt as gross as mine, the penalty had already been paid. I began to see the power of God's love to overcome death and destruction, His power to heal it, not just abstractly but immediately and specifically—for me."

Anyone who visits Tex Watson will see that Jesus Christ is real, immediately and specifically real. However much the church may have failed Him, Christ's revolutionary power has not diminished in the least. He is still creating the kingdom of God today—in the most unlikely places, among the most hopeless cases.

And this crucified, resurrected Saviour is eager to have a life-changing encounter with *you* today. Have you made your personal commitment to the cross, to the Lord who rose from the grave?

The Bible says this about Jesus: "Who Himself bore our sins in His own body on the tree, that we, having died to sins, might live for righteousness—by whose stripes you were healed. For you were like sheep going astray, but have

now returned to the Shepherd and Overseer of your souls"
(1 Peter 2:24, 25, NKJV).

Christ's peace in our hearts will transform us, leading us
to turn from sin and live unto righteousness.

The story is told of a new Christian whose faith in the
Bible was challenged by his former drinking buddies. "We
don't believe Jesus really turned water into wine," they
scoffed. "How do you know such a miracle really happened?"

For a moment the new believer wondered what to say.
Then he quietly replied, "I admit I can't prove Jesus turned
water into wine two thousand years ago. But I can tell you
this. In our home He turned my six-packs of beer into
furniture for my family!"

Praise God, He can work miracles in your heart and in
your home too, through the power of the Lord Jesus Christ.
The decision is yours to make. I plead with you not to delay
it. Time is short, and life is uncertain. Six shattering
seconds took America's healthy young president through
the doorway of death. Who knows what the future holds for
you? You can find new peace and security as you place your
life in the hands of Christ as we pray.

* * *

*"Heavenly Father, each of us is individually responsible
for the death of Jesus. But we don't have to feel sad about it.
No, we can lift up our hearts and rejoice in Your forgiveness.
Thank You, dear Lord, for caring so much that You gave us
Your Son so we could be saved. Your love for us is real. Now
help us to know also how real Your commitment to us is.
Thank You. In Christ's saving name we pray. Amen."*

More Than a Hostage

They had endured years of imprisonment, isolation, and sometimes outright brutality. But the faces that emerged from "somewhere in Lebanon" didn't quite fit the part. They didn't seem broken by their long ordeal as hostages. Their broad smiles and easy laughter spoke of something entirely different. What was the secret for these cheerful survivors?

When Terry Anderson, the last American hostage in Lebanon, was finally freed in December 1991, he and his companions were able at last to tell their harrowing story. The picture that emerged made it difficult to see how any of them had survived those years with their sanity intact. They told of airless, windowless cells barely larger than a grave. Extremes of heat in the day and cold at night. The same clothes year after year. Filthy blindfolds that infected their eyes. Steel chains unlocked only once a day during their ten-minute toilet visit to a hole in the ground. Just enough food to keep body and soul together—usually eaten alone in the dark.

Almost all the hostages were beaten, some so severely that they are permanently injured. Terry Anderson recalls one terrible night hearing a hostage with pneumonia in the next cell—choking to death on his own fluids.

Anglican Church envoy Terry Waite was kept in total and complete isolation for four years. He suffered from a serious asthma condition—yet he emerged with what one reporter called a "megawatt smile," joking good-heartedly with Lord Runcie, his former boss. Terry Anderson also seemed amazingly fit—both physically and emotionally.

Reporters who talked to the hostages after their release often commented on how remarkably well they seemed to have survived their ordeal. As they appeared on our TV screens, we saw no nervous gestures or blank gazes—none of the telltale signs of those who've been scarred by suffering and isolation.

How did so many of them survive so well? That was the question on everyone's mind. What lay behind their bouncy steps and wide grins? As more and more of the hostage experience came to light, so did the secret.

Terry Anderson had been raised in church, but traveling the world as a reporter, he'd pretty much left his faith behind. During captivity, a fellow hostage and clergyman, Pastor Lawrence Jenco, counseled Anderson in his dark moments. They talked about spiritual things—and the reporter rediscovered his faith. Anderson began praying regularly. He learned that, even in the midst of grueling isolation, God could still be a comforting companion.

What sustained Anderson through 2,455 days of captivity? He said it was the Bible and a picture of his daughter, whom he'd never seen, that got him through.

French hostage Roger Auque made a similar discovery. After his release, he said simply, "Before, I didn't believe in God, and now I do."

Hostage Benjamin Weir looked up in his cell one day and noticed three bare wires hanging from the ceiling. For some reason those wires suggested to him the extended fingers of God in one of Michelangelo's paintings in the Sistine Chapel. Pastor Weir recalls, "That became to me a representation of the sustaining, purposeful hand of God."

Faith blossomed in those dark cells in Lebanon. Lonely men found the strength to survive. The secret behind their survival and their good spirits when released was what the hostages called their "Church of the Locked Door." They conducted regular Christian services, using bits of bread to celebrate Communion. They kept their faith alive, and faith kept them alive.

Even their guards could, at times, respect this kind of resilient belief. On Christmas Day 1985, several hostages received a cake while two Muslim guards sang in broken English, "Happy Birthday, Jesus."

The message these courageous hostages give to us reminds me of another message written long ago. Do you know what the most joyful book in the Bible is? It's Paul's letter to the Philippians. That short letter just brims over with the joy of a man whose faith is simply unsinkable. And what makes it all the more remarkable is that this letter was written from prison. Paul sent out this wonderfully encouraging letter while he himself was guarded by Roman soldiers. Like the hostages in Lebanon, Paul also demonstrated that faith in Jesus Christ can make us content, even joyful, in any circumstances.

What is faith? How do you define it? Is faith believing that God is going to send you a thousand dollars in the mail to help pay the monthly bills? Is it believing it won't rain because you want to go on a family picnic? Is it confidence that God will heal your husband or wife dying of cancer? Just what is this quality called faith? Perhaps you've always thought of faith as a sort of refuge for the weak or a crutch of last resort—when all else fails, you try to have faith.

Biblical faith is confidence in God. It is trusting God as a well-known friend, believing that in every situation He has your best interest in mind. Faith is Job suffering from head to toe with boils—losing his home, family, and source of livelihood—still able to declare: " 'Though He slay me, yet will I trust Him' " (Job 13:15, NKJV).

Faith is Daniel, a hostage in a foreign land, determining to be loyal to God in the face of immense pressure. Faith is Jesus hanging on the cross with blood running down His face, triumphantly proclaiming, " 'Father, into your hands I commit my spirit' " (Luke 23:46).

Faith grows as we come into contact with its source in God's Word. The more we know God, the more confidence we have in Him. We get to know Him by studying His Word.

I want to assure you that faith is the *first* thing we need in this life, not the last. Faith is how we grow as healthy human beings, not just how we face death or disaster. The hostages in Lebanon simply demonstrated that faith works even in the worst of circumstances. They tested it in the fiery furnace and found it came out as pure gold.

Listen to Paul, the joyful apostle, describe how faith enables us to face difficulties. "Take up the shield of faith, with which you can extinguish all the flaming arrows of the evil one" (Ephesians 6:16). We live in a world where bad things happen. Life is a struggle. But we don't have to go out there afraid and vulnerable. Paul tells us that faith is a great shield. We can go into battle well armed. Faith extinguishes all the flaming arrows of the evil one.

There are not many things in this life that do that. Getting a new car or moving into a new house won't do it. Having a good job won't do it. All the success and prosperity in the world won't do it. Even with all these things, we're still basically vulnerable, insecure human beings. We can still get shot through—right to the heart.

But faith does extinguish those arrows Satan throws at us. Faith in Jesus Christ, a relationship with Him, is like a shield around us. We can take whatever life may throw our way.

The hostages came out of their long ordeal as winners, not losers. I believe their faith had a lot to do with that. The apostle John tells us that faith makes people winners. "This is the victory that has overcome the world, even our faith" (1 John 5:4). Faith overcomes the world, that is, the evil in the world. Faith is stronger than life's tragedies. It can make us winners.

There is a reason that New Testament writers sometimes refer to "the world" as something that needs to be overcome. "The world" is often used as a symbol of a society in rebellion against God, of people who try to live apart from Him. From the Bible's perspective, there's very little neutral ground on this planet. You're either guided by a loving heavenly Father, or you're under the control of someone else.

The Scriptures are very plain about who is in control of this world today. The book of Revelation identifies Satan as the one "who leads the whole world astray" (Revelation 12:9). The devil is pictured as playing a very active role on this planet. Anyone who has taken a glance through a history book knows about man's inhumanity to man. At times, human cruelty is overwhelming. That's why the apostle John could exclaim in his epistle: "We know that . . . the whole world is under the control of the evil one" (1 John 5:19).

In other words, we're all hostages. An evil power has taken over our home. We can't comprehend why the wars have to go on and on, why bigotry and injustice and greed multiply like infectious diseases. But they do. They surround us. We're hostages in a world where Satan has all but taken over. So the experience of those men imprisoned in Lebanon speaks to us; it echoes in miniature our wider predicament.

And as we all know, there are days when that predicament seems just too much. Terry Anderson had such a day.

It was Christmas Day 1986. No communication had been allowed between hostages for some time. They had no books, nothing to read. But Anderson had learned sign language in high school, the one-handed alphabet. And he managed to secretly teach it to the others. In this way they were able to relay messages down the line. But on this Christmas Day he took off his glasses, dropped them, and broke them. Anderson had such poor eyesight that he could no longer see what his companions were signing. He was cut off once again.

Isolation is a terrible thing. It's bad enough to be a hostage, but being a hostage alone—that's all but unbearable. You know, that's exactly what our enemy Satan is trying to do to us. His strategy is to cut us off from our heavenly Father, to break down the lines of communication. He knows that once we're isolated from God, he can break us.

There are many ways in which our spiritual glasses can fall off and break. Many things can prevent us from seeing God nearby. Guilt, emotional trauma, bitterness, or just plain indifference can all sever that essential line of communication.

That's why it's so important for us to fight back. As hostages on a planet in rebellion against God, we can't just go with the flow, because the flow takes us away from God. We have to fight against the things that separate us from our heavenly Father. Paul warns us, "Our struggle is not against flesh and blood, but against the rulers, against the authorities, against the powers of this dark world" (Ephesians 6:12).

Evil forces are at work around us. And Paul is telling us: Don't just lie down and be a casualty; fight back, join the good fight of faith. We've got to lay claim to our rights as children of God, or we'll become just another victim of the cruelty of this world.

The guards in Lebanon seemed to take particular delight in tormenting Father Lawrence Jenco, a Catholic priest. Once, a man in copper-tipped cowboy boots began stepping on his head. Something welled up inside this priest. He shouted, "I am not an insect! I am a person of worth!" While in captivity, Father Jenco had kept those lines of communication with God open. He knew who he was, and he would not behave like an animal, even though he was treated like one.

His cries of protest were a way of fighting back. He was saying: "I am more than a hostage. I am more than this prisoner in your hands."

Friends, that's what we need to say: "I am more than just a hostage. I may be surrounded by cruelty and indifference in this world, but I won't give in and become a part of it."

How do we do that? By doing what the hostages did: They nurtured their faith; they held on to it. They maintained a personal relationship with their heavenly Father.

Faith in the Lord Jesus Christ is a powerful force in this world. Never underestimate it. Faith is leverage; it's how we rise above our circumstances. It's the only way we can become more than hostages on this planet.

These remarkable prisoners in Lebanon had another important element in their strategy of survival. They made sure that their world did not shrink to the size of their cells. They made sure their minds were filled with something bigger and better than what they could see in captivity.

When they could communicate a bit, each hostage would try to take the others on an elaborate, imaginary tour of some city he knew well. Father Jenco served as a knowledgeable guide through Rome. Terry Anderson took them through Tokyo. Benjamin Weir described parts of Lebanon or Turkey.

The men lived for news from the outside. On those occasions when Terry Anderson was able to listen to radio reports, he would tap out dispatches to the others on world events. He would tap once for *a*, twice for *b*, three times for *c*, and so on. It took an incredible amount of time just to get one sentence across. But that precious glimpse of what they regarded as the "real world" was worth it.

Those men in tiny, dark cells somewhere in Lebanon were more than hostages because they focused on what was waiting for them on the outside. We need the same perspective. Peter explains in his first letter:

> In his great mercy he has given us new birth into a living hope through the resurrection of Jesus Christ from the dead, and into an inheritance that can never perish, spoil or fade—kept in heaven for you, who through faith are shielded by God's power until the coming of the salvation that is ready to be revealed in the last time (1 Peter 1:3-5).

All those who've been born again by faith can find great strength in their real connection to another "real world." We have an inheritance that can never spoil or fade. We have a home in heaven waiting for us. The connection with God that we nurture now, sometimes with real struggle, will someday be revealed as a glorious, physical reality.

Peter says "through faith" we are "shielded by God's power" until the coming of salvation, the second coming of Christ. Again, it is faith that enables us to make it through. Faith enables us to live a healthy life even on a planet held hostage by the enemy. Faith helps us survive in good spirits, and faith helps us focus on the "real world," the home God is preparing for us.

Speaking of the great hope of a coming salvation, Peter goes on to say:

In this you greatly rejoice, though now for a little while you may have had to suffer grief in all kinds of trials. These have come so that your faith—of greater worth than gold . . . may be proved genuine and may result in praise, glory and honor when Jesus Christ is revealed (1 Peter 1:6, 7).

Yes, we do have pain and sadness in this life. Believers are not immune from tragedy. But something good can come out of trial. Our faith can become as precious as gold. And faith will find its ultimate reward when Christ is revealed. Peter goes on to say that, even if we don't see Jesus now, our faith can produce "an inexpressible and glorious joy" (verse 8).

Why?

Because we know where we're going. We know what lies ahead. Hope is not just grasping at straws when it is a hope based in Jesus Christ. Faith connects us to that other very real world from which Jesus will soon appear.

The hostages in Lebanon hung on to their faith, and they were wonderfully rewarded. We all rejoiced with them when they were finally able to rush to the arms of loved ones and that outside "real world" became a glorious, physical reality for them. The tiny photographs they had clutched to their hearts in the cramped darkness now became talking, laughing, weeping, flesh-and-blood people. Those were wonderful reunions.

I'm looking forward to some wonderful reunions too. I'm looking forward to gazing into the faces of loved ones who have passed away. I'm longing for the day when I can look into the face of the Lord Jesus Christ. Won't that be wonderful? Our faith will be triumphant and inexpressibly joyous then.

Yes, we are more than hostages. We're not just victims of

the cruelty and indifference of this planet. We are children of God, claimed by Him, about to be taken to a heavenly home by Him.

Are you feeling like a hostage today? Have you been having one of those dark days or weeks when life seems just too much to handle? Why not begin fighting back today, right now? Why not make a stand with the One who laid down His life so you could be more than a hostage? A relationship with Him can get you through the hard times in good spirits. You can survive as a healthy human being. You can have a living hope in an inheritance that will never spoil or fade.

* * *

"Father, we need Your rescue today. We know that we have often lived as hostages to the principalities and powers of this world. We've been held captive to evil desires. But we want to be more than hostages now. We want to take our place as Your children. Thank You for making our escape possible by Your sacrifice on the cross. Thank You for offering us pardon and the power to live a new life. We commit ourselves to You as Saviour and Lord, Amen."

Joy in the Morning

It was Friday. Dark, dark Friday. He was tried on Friday. Condemned on Friday. Crucified on Friday. The sun hid its face on Friday. Birds hushed their songs. Flowers veiled their faces. The entire face of the earth wept that Friday.

Judas betrayed Him. Peter denied Him. And each of the disciples forsook Him. All alone, He was taken from the quiet garden in Gethsemane. Beaten. Oppressed. Flogged. The crown of thorns was jammed upon His head. Blood ran down His face. He was spiked to a wooden cross. A spear wound left a gaping hole in His side as He hung on that cross with nails in His hands. Then that final cry of triumph—"It is finished!" And black clouds hid the final scene. It was a dark Friday.

Over the Sabbath He rested in death as He had rested in life. His disciples hid themselves away in a dimly lighted upper room in Jerusalem, their tears interrupted only by their words of discouragement and doubt and doom. Everything they had lived for was gone. When Christ died that Friday, their hopes were dashed like a bottle thrown against the wall and broken to pieces. The Messiah was gone.

Those eleven men had walked away from their nets,

their fishing boats, their tax-collecting tables to follow Him.
They had left behind their occupations and families and
friends to follow a Man whom they believed to be the
Saviour of the world.

Now, defeated, locked in an upper room, they cowered in
fear with the window blacked out and a guard at the door.
Questions loomed large. "Will His fate become our fate
too?" "Will His destiny become our doom?" "What does the
future hold?" Their Messiah was dead.

Early that Sunday morning, two of those disciples decided to go to the tomb. The Scripture says:

> Now upon the first day of the week, very early
> in the morning, they came unto the sepulchre,
> bringing the spices which they had prepared,
> and certain others with them. And they found
> the stone rolled away from the sepulchre. And
> they entered in, and found not the body of the
> Lord Jesus. And it came to pass, as they were
> much perplexed thereabout, behold, two men
> stood by them in shining garments: And as they
> were afraid, and bowed down their faces to the
> earth, they said unto them, Why seek ye the
> living among the dead? He is not here, but is
> risen (Luke 24:1-6, KJV).

He is risen. Three words that have changed the universe.
He is risen. Black Friday has become glorious Sunday!
There is joy in the morning. Their sorrow turns to gladness
and rejoicing.

The birds sang that morning. The flowers appeared more
beautiful that morning. The sun shone in a magnificent,
cloudless sky that morning. There was joy in the morning.
Christ was risen from the dead! Christ was alive!

Filled with that joy, these disciples could hardly contain

themselves. They were electrified by the news of the risen Christ, transformed from fearful saints to confident believers. They left the tomb running. Approaching the upper room where the other disciples were hidden in fear, the two banged on the door. They could hardly wait to enter, shouting, "He is risen! He is risen! We have seen the Lord!" There was joy in the morning.

When the disciples grasped the significance of Jesus' resurrection, they spread the good news everywhere. The resurrection proved Jesus to be divine. No human has power over the grave. No mere man could raise himself from the dead. The prophecies focusing on the life, death, and resurrection of Christ were true. The disciples were gripped with the marvelous fact that Jesus truly is the Son of God.

His resurrection makes all the difference for you and me too. We're not left alone here in this world to fight against the forces of evil by ourselves. Christianity is not some ideology; it's not some philosophy. It's not some dogma demanding merely intellectual or mental assent. Christianity is the belief in a *Person*—the person of Jesus Christ, the divine Son of God, who existed with the Father from eternity.

Christ broke into human history to reveal the Father's love. He died on the cross to provide salvation for you and for me. And He is resurrected from the dead. He is alive! And because He is, He can turn our dark Fridays into joyful resurrection mornings. Because He's alive, He can turn our sadness into joy. Because He's alive, He can wipe the tears from our eyes.

Every one of us has dark Fridays. We have times when our body is filled with pain. We have times when our friends forsake us, when we feel terribly alone. There are times when we feel depressed and discouraged. We all have our dark Fridays.

Maybe you're going through a dark Friday right now. Possibly you are reading this book while sick, and your body is hurting. Maybe you've been diagnosed with cancer. Maybe you've just experienced coronary bypass surgery. Perhaps your entire body is in pain with an arthritic condition. You may have just gone through an auto accident or some other painful affliction.

Maybe you have gone through the emotional agony of a divorce. Your husband has left you for another woman. Your wife has run out on you. And you go to bed every night crying. You are right now in a dark Friday.

Maybe you're a teenager, and your friends don't seem to care. Your boyfriend or girlfriend has broken up with you. Or you've flunked some exam at school. You're going through a dark Friday.

It could be financial difficulty. Bills that you hadn't expected have come crashing down on you. You are experiencing your dark Friday. But Christ is alive! And this living Christ cares for you. The Bible assures you that this living Christ knows your problems, understands your difficulties, and wants to minister healing and hope and encouragement to your heart. Listen:

> Because He continues forever . . . He is also able to save to the uttermost those who come to God through Him, since He ever lives to make intercession for them (Hebrews 7:24, 25, NKJV).

He lives to make intercession for you. Your name is on His lips. Your problems bring Him concern. Your difficulties are lodged in His heart. Anything that perplexes you perplexes Him. Even the brokenness of your life can be an instrument that God uses to make you a more beautiful person.

Many years ago, when the royal Muslim mosque was

being built in Tehran, the exquisite building was designed to have a foyer lined with magnificent cut-glass mirrors. The idea was that the sun would shine down upon these cut-glass mirrors through an open dome in the top of the foyer. The mirrors would reflect magnificent rainbow colors throughout the marbled entryway. The hand-cut mirrors were magnificently and exquisitely designed in Italy and then flown to Iran.

They arrived at the workplace just in time to be put into the foyer, when it was discovered that they were terribly damaged and cracked. The workmen stood aghast. Then a master artist told them to take their hammers and crack the mirrors even more. Now the workmen were really astounded. The mirrors that were already damaged were to be cracked further?

They did as they were told, however, and once they were finished, the artist told them to prepare fresh cement. Then he carefully began placing the jagged pieces of broken glass in the fresh cement in the foyer of the royal mosque.

If you were to visit there today, you would see the light streaming through the dome, reflecting on each individual bit of glass, making the foyer exquisite. It appears as if you are standing in acres of diamonds. Somebody said, "The glass was broken so that the foyer would become more beautiful, an honor to God."

Maybe you feel your life is like those broken mirrors. But I have good news for you. Christ is risen! There are dark Fridays, but there is a glorious Sunday too. A day of resurrection and rebirth. If your life has been broken, it's been broken only to be made more beautiful for the Saviour's cause and for His name.

The dark Friday of the crucifixion became transformed into the glorious resurrection morning. And because Christ is risen, we can have new life with Him—both here in this world and in the world to come. Paul says, "You died, and your life is hidden with Christ in God. When Christ who is our life appears, then you also will appear with Him in glory" (Colossians 3:3, 4, NKJV).

The promise is sure. Because Christ died and is risen, salvation is yours for the asking. Won't you ask Him to give you His new life—His resurrection life—now as we pray?

* * *

"Father, we are so grateful that our dark Fridays can be transformed into a glorious new life in Christ. Take our old lives with their sins and their pain. We give them to You. Turn our sorrow into joy. Cover us with the salvation Jesus has provided on the cross so that when He appears, we will appear with Him in glory to live forever with You. Thank You, in the name of Jesus. Amen."